Traditional Irish Favourites

23 classic songs for keyboard

© International Music Publications Ltd
First published in 1996 by International Music Publications Ltd
International Music Publications Ltd is a Faber Music company
Bloomsbury House 74–77 Great Russell Street London WC1B 3DA
Music arranged & processed by Barnes Music Engraving Ltd
Cover Image © Digital Vision
Printed in England by Caligraving Ltd
All rights reserved

ISBN10: 0-571-52881-3
EAN13: 978-0-571-52881-3

DANNY BOY
(LONDONDERRY AIR)

Traditional

Suggested Registration: Strings
Rhythm: Soft Rock
Tempo: ♩ = 104

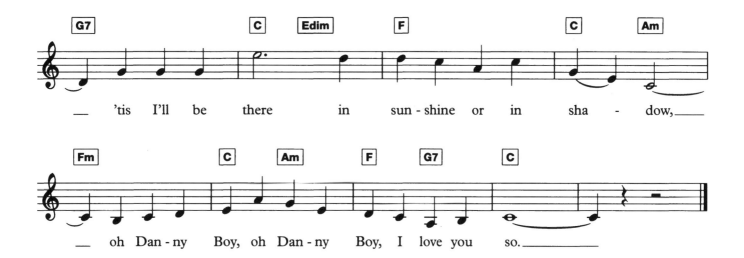

'tis I'll be there in sun-shine or in sha - dow,____

__ oh Dan-ny Boy, oh Dan-ny Boy, I love you so._____

1   Oh Danny Boy, the pipes, the pipes are calling,
From glen to glen and down the mountainside.
The summer's gone, and all the roses falling,
'Tis you, 'tis you must go, and I must bide.
But come ye back when summer's in the meadow,
Or when the valley's hushed and white with snow,
'Tis I'll be there in sunshine or in shadow,
Oh Danny Boy, oh Danny Boy, I love you so.

2   And when ye come, and all the flowers are dying,
If I am dead, as dead I well may be,
You'll come and find the place where I am lying,
And kneel and say an 'Ave' there for me.
And I shall hear though soft you tread above me,
And all my grave will warmer, sweeter be.
If you will bend, and tell me that you love me,
Then I shall sleep in peace until you come to me.

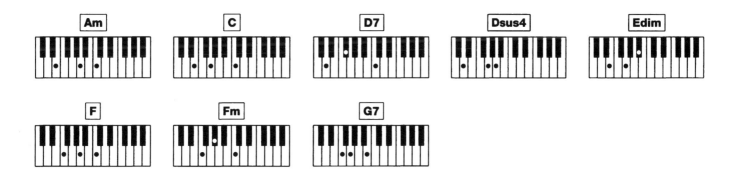

THE DEAR LITTLE SHAMROCK

Traditional

Suggested Registration: Acoustic Guitar V43 DV7o D
Rhythm: Waltz
Tempo: ♩ = 108   S191 (T108)

There's a dear lit-tle plant that grows in our Isle, 'twas Saint Pat-rick him-self sure that set it,___ and the sun on his la-bour with plea-sure did smile, and the dew from his eye of-ten wet it.___ It shines through the bog, through the brake, through the mire-land, and he called it the dear lit-tle Sham-rock of

Ire - land. The dear lit - tle Sham - rock, the sweet lit - tle

Sham-rock, the dear lit - tle, sweet lit - tle Sham - rock of Ire - land.

1   There's a dear little plant that grows in our Isle,
    'Twas Saint Patrick himself sure that set it,
    And the sun on his labour with pleasure did smile,
    And the dew from his eye often wet it.
    It shines through the bog, through the brake, through the mireland,
    And he called it the dear little Shamrock of Ireland.
        The dear little Shamrock, the sweet little Shamrock,
        The dear little, sweet little Shamrock of Ireland.

2   That dear little plant still grows in our land,
    Fresh and fair as the daughters of Erin,
    Whose smiles can bewitch, and whose eyes can command,
    In each climate they ever appear in.
    For they shine through the bog, through the brake, through the mireland,
    Just like their own dear little Shamrock of Ireland.
        The dear little Shamrock . . .

3   That dear little plant that springs from our soil,
    When its three little leaves are extended,
    Denotes from the the stalk we together should toil,
    And ourselves by ourselves be befriended.
    And still through the bog, through the brake, through the mireland,
    From one root should branch, like the Shamrock of Ireland.
        The dear little Shamrock . . .

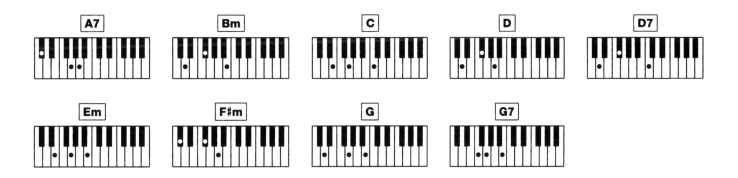

Delaney's Donkey

Words and Music by William Hargreaves

Suggested Registration: Accordian
Rhythm: Shuffle
Tempo: ♩ = 112

don - key was eye-ing them, o - pen-ly de-fy - ing them, wink-ing, blink-ing, twist-ing out of place.

Ri - ley re-vers-ing it, ev-ery-bo - dy curs-ing it, the day De-la-ney's don-key ran the half-mile race.

1   Delaney had a donkey everyone admired,
    Tempo'rily lazy, permanently tired;
    A leg at every corner balancing its head,
    And a tail to let you know which end it wanted to be fed.
    Riley slyly said, 'We've underrated it. Why not train it?'
    Then he took a rag, rubbed it, scrubbed it, oiled and embrocated it,
    Got it to the post, and when the starter dropped the flag:

> *There was Riley pushing it, shoving it and shushing it,*
> *Hogan, Logan, everyone in town,*
> *Lined up attacking it, shoving it and smacking it;*
> *They might as well have tried to push the Town Hall down.*
> *The donkey was eyeing them, openly defying them,*
> *Winking, blinking, twisting out of place,*
> *Riley reversing it, everybody cursing it,*
> *The day Delaney's donkey ran the half-mile race.*

2   The muscles of the mighty, never known to flinch,
    Didn't move the donkey quarter of an inch.
    Delaney lay exhausted, hanging round its throat,
    With a grip just like a Scotchman on a twenty shilling note.
    Starter, Carter, lined up all the rest of 'em;
    When it saw them, it was willing then.
    Raced up, braced up, ready for the best of 'em;
    They started off to cheer it,
        but it changed its mind again.

> *There was Riley pushing it, shoving it and shushing it,*
> *Hogan, Logan, Mary Ann Macgraw.*
> *She started poking it, grabbing it and choking it;*
> *It kicked her in the bustle, and it laughed, 'Hee-Haw!'*
> *The whigs and conservatives, radical superlatives,*
> *Lib'rals, tories, hurried to the place,*
> *Stood there in unity, helping the community,*
> *To push Delaney's donkey in the half-mile race.*

3   The crowd began to cheer it, Rafferty, the judge,
    Came up to assist them, still it wouldn't budge.
    The jockey who was riding, little John MacGee,
    Was so thoroughly disgusted he went home to get his tea.
    Hagan, Fagan, students of psychology,
    Swore they'd shift it with some dynamite;
    Bought it, brought it, then without apology,
    The donkey gave a sneeze,
        and blew the darn stuff out of sight.

> *There was Riley pushing it, shoving it, and shushing it,*
> *Hogan, Logan, all the bally crew,*
> *P'lice and auxil'ary, the Garrison Artillery,*
> *The Second Inniskillings, and the Life Guards too.*
> *They seized it, and harried it, picked it up and carried it,*
> *Cheered it, steered it to the winning place.*
> *Bookies all drew aside and committed suicide,*
> *Because Delaney's donkey won the half-mile race.*

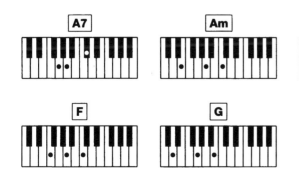

Dublin Bay

Words by Mrs Crawford / Music by George Barker

Suggested Registration: Accordian
Rhythm: Slow Rock 6/8
Tempo: ♩ = 52

1 He sailed away in a gallant bark,
Roy Neill and his fair young bride.
He had ventured all in that bounding oak,
That danced o'er the silver tide.
But his heart was young, and his spirit light,
And he dashed the tear away,
As he watched the shores recede from sight,
Of his own sweet Dublin Bay.

2 Three days they sailed, and a storm arose
And the lightning swept the deep,
And the thunder crash broke the short repose
Of the weary seaboy's sleep.
Roy Neill, he clasped his weeping bride,
And kissed her tears away.
'Oh love, 'twas a fatal hour', she cried,
'When we left Dublin Bay.'

3 On the crowded deck of the doomed ship,
Some stood in mute despair,
And some, more calm, with a holy lip,
Sought the God of the storm in prayer.
'She has struck on the rocks!' the seamen cried,
In the breath of their wild dismay,
And the ship went down, and the fair young bride,
That sailed from Dublin Bay.

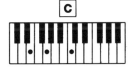
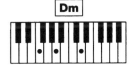
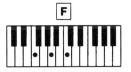
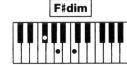

Galway Bay

Words and Music by Dr Arthur Colahan

Suggested Registration: Piano
Rhythm: Soft Rock
Tempo: ♩ = 96

Vi DV95
S130 (T140)
S128 (T96)

If you ev-er go a-cross the sea to

Ire - land, then may-be at the clos-ing of your day, you will

sit and watch the moon rise o - ver Clad-dagh, and see the sun go down on Gal-way

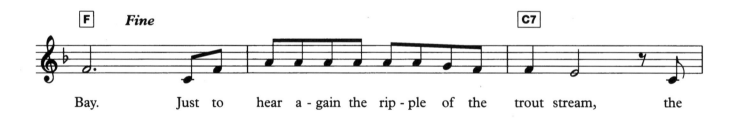

Bay. Just to hear a-gain the rip-ple of the trout stream, the

wo - men in the mea-dows mak-ing hay, and to

sit be - side a turf fire in the cab - in, and

watch the bare - foot Gos - soons at their play.

1   If you ever go across the sea to Ireland,
Then maybe at the closing of your day,
You will sit and watch the moon rise over Claddagh,
And see the sun go down on Galway Bay.
Just to hear again the ripple of the trout stream,
The women in the meadows making hay,
And to sit beside a turf fire in the cabin,
And watch the barefoot Gossoons at their play.

2   For the breezes blowing o'er the seas from Ireland,
Are perfumed by the heather as they blow,
And the women in the uplands diggin' praties,
Speak a language that the strangers do not know.
For the strangers came and tried to teach us their way,
They scorned us just for being what we are,
But they might as well go chasing after moonbeams,
Or light a penny candle from a star.

And if there is going to be a life hereafter,
And somehow I am sure there's going to be,
I will ask my God to let me make my heaven,
In that dear land across the Irish Sea.

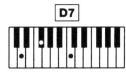
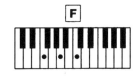
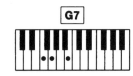

The Harp That Once

Words by Thomas Moore / Music traditional

Suggested Registration: Flute V137 DV.105 S45 (T76)
Rhythm: Soft Rock S 191 (T108)
Tempo: ♩ = 108

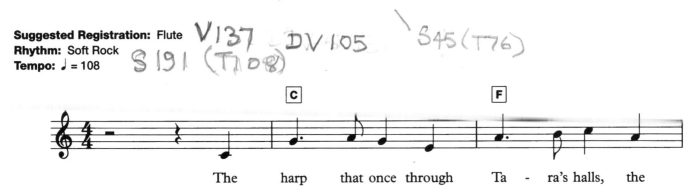

The   harp   that once through   Ta - ra's halls,   the

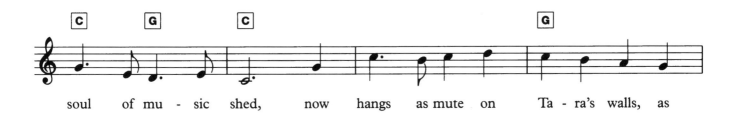

soul   of mu - sic   shed,   now   hangs   as mute   on   Ta - ra's   walls,   as

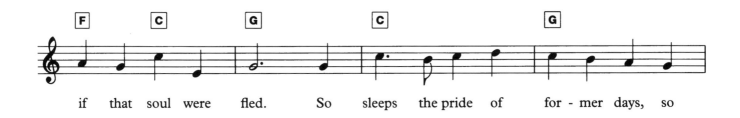

if   that   soul   were   fled.   So   sleeps   the pride   of   for - mer days,   so

glo - ry's   thrill   is   o'er;   and   hearts   that once   beat

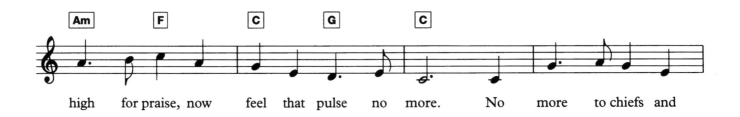

high   for praise, now   feel   that pulse   no   more.   No   more   to chiefs   and

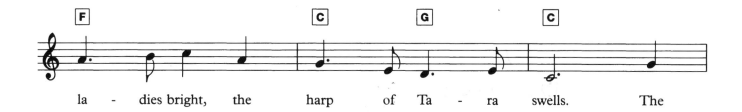

la - dies bright, the harp of Ta - ra swells. The

chord a - lone that breaks the night, its tale of ru - in

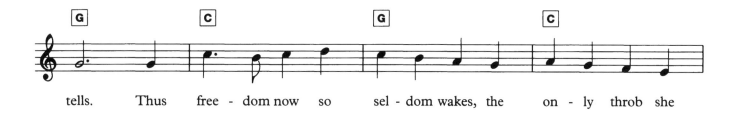

tells. Thus free - dom now so sel - dom wakes, the on - ly throb she

gives, is when some heart in - dig - nant breaks, to show that she still lives.

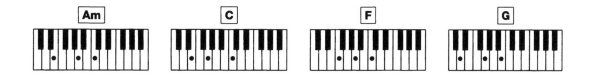

HOW CAN YOU BUY KILLARNEY?

Words and Music by Hamilton Kennedy, Freddie Grant, Gerald Morrison and Ted Steels

Suggested Registration: Violin
Rhythm: Slow Rock 6/8
Tempo: ♩. = 60

gifts with a smile. The em - 'rald, the sham - rock, the blar - ney.

When you can buy all these won-der-ful things, Then you can buy Kil - lar - ney.'

1   An American landed on Erin's green isle,
He gazed at Killarney with rapturous smile,
'How can I buy it?' said he to his guide,
'I'll tell you how,' with a smile, he replied.
    'How can you buy all the stars in the skies?
    How can you buy two blue Irish eyes?
    How can you purchase a fond mother's sighs?
    How can you buy Killarney?
    Nature bestowed all her gifts with a smile.
    The em'rald, the shamrock, the blarney.
    When you can buy all these wonderful things,
    Then you can buy Killarney.'

2   Such a wonderful landscape, you never have seen,
A jewel so rare, 'twould befit any queen.
Pride of Erin, a joy to behold,
Heaven on earth, far more precious than gold.
    'How can you buy . . .'

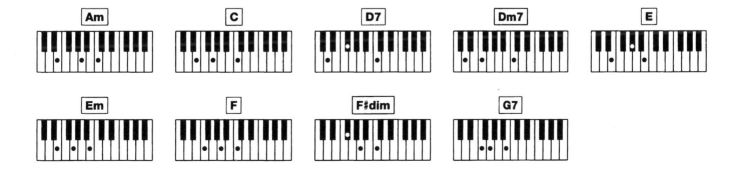

I'll Take You Home Again, Kathleen

Traditional

Suggested Registration: 'Cello
Rhythm: Soft Rock
Tempo: ♩ = 84

- leen,   to   where   your heart will feel no   pain,   and   when   the fields are fresh and

green,   I'll___   take   you   to   your home   a - gain.

1   I'll take you home again Kathleen,
Across the ocean wild and wide,
To where your heart has ever been,
Since first you were my bonny bride.
The roses have all left your cheek.
I've watched them fade away and die.
Your voice is sad whene'er you speak,
And tears bedim your loving eyes.
   Oh! I will take you back Kathleen,
   To where your heart will feel no pain,
   And when the fields are fresh and green,
   I'll take you to your home again.

2   I know you love me, Kathleen dear,
Your heart was ever fond and true.
I always feel when you are near,
That life holds nothing, dear, but you.
The smiles that once you gave to me,
I scarcely ever see them now.
Though many, many times I see,
A darkening shadow on your brow.
   Oh! I will take . . .

3   To that dear home beyond the sea,
My Kathleen shall again return,
And when thy old friends welcome thee,
Thy loving heart will cease to yearn.
Where laughs the little silver stream,
Beside your master's humble cot,
And brightest rays of sunshine gleam,
There, all your grief will be forgot.
   Oh! I will take . . .

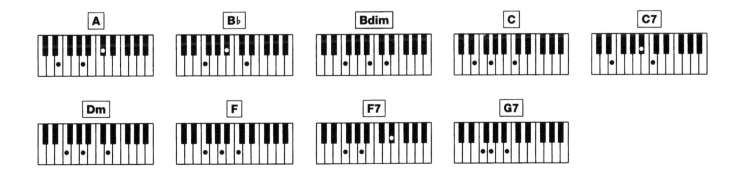

If You're Irish
Come Into The Parlour

Words and Music by Shaun Glenville and Frank Miller

Suggested Registration: Piano
Rhythm: Shuffle
Tempo: ♩ = 104

If you're I - rish____ come in - to the par -

- lour, there's a wel - come there for you.____

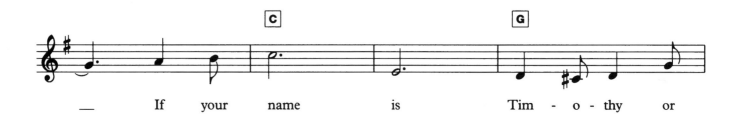

_ If your name is Tim - o - thy or

Pat,____ so long as you come from Ire - land, there's a

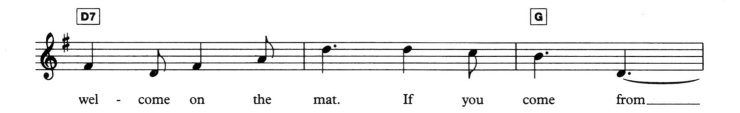

wel - come on the mat. If you come from____

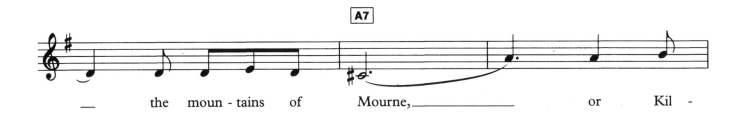

the moun-tains of Mourne,_____ or Kil-

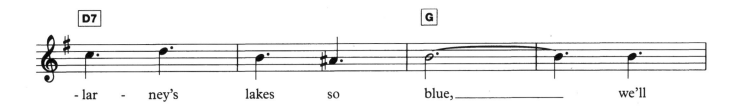

-lar - ney's lakes so blue,_____ we'll

sing you a song, and we'll make a fuss, who-

-ev - er you are, you are one of us, if you're I - rish,

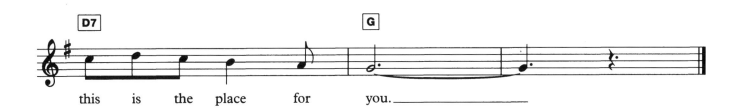

this is the place for you._____

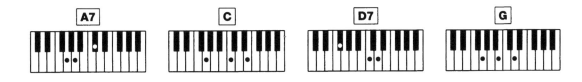

THE IRISH ROVER

Traditional

Suggested Registration: Accordian
Rhythm: Soft Rock
Tempo: ♩ = 100

V35 JV95
S148 (T200) S193(T200)

In the year of our Lord, eight-een hun-dred and six, we set
sail from the coal quay of Cork. We were sail-ing a-way with a
car-go of bricks, for the grand ci-ty hall in New York. We'd an
e-le-gant craft, it was rigged fore and aft, and how the trade winds
drove_____ her. She had twen-ty-three masts, and she
stood sev-eral blasts, and they called her the I-rish Ro-ver.

1   In the year of our Lord, eighteen hundred and six,
    We set sail from the coal quay of Cork.
    We were sailing away with a cargo of bricks,
    For the grand city hall in New York.
    We'd an elegant craft, it was rigged fore and aft,
    And how the trade winds drove her.
    She had twenty-three masts, and she stood several blasts,
    And they called her the Irish Rover.

2   There was Barney Magee from the banks of the Lee,
    There was Hogan from County Tyrone,
    There was Johnny McGurk who was scared stiff of work,
    And a chap from Westmeath named Malone.
    There was Slugger O'Toole, who drank as a rule,
    And fighting Bill Tracy from Dover,
    And your man Mick McCann, from the banks of the Bann,
    Was the skipper on the Irish Rover.

3   We had one million bags of the best Sligo rags,
    We had two million barrels of bone,
    We had three million bales of old nanny goats' tails,
    We had four million barrels of stone.
    We had five million hogs and six million dogs,
    And seven million barrels of porter,
    We had eight million sides of old horses' hides,
    In the hold of the Irish Rover.

4   We had sailed seven years when the measles broke out,
    And our ship lost her way in a fog,
    And the whole of the crew was reduced down to two,
    'Twas myself and the captain's old dog.
    Then the ship struck a rock, oh Lord, what a shock,
    And nearly tumbled over,
    Turned nine times around, then the poor dog was drowned.
    I'm the last of the Irish Rover.

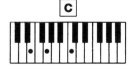

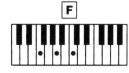

The Isle Of Innisfree

Words and Music by Dick Farrelly

Suggested Registration: Flute   V137 DV 105
Rhythm: Soft Rock
Tempo: ♩ = 96   S128 (T96)

I've met some folks who say that I'm a

dream-er, and I've no doubt there's truth in what they say, but sure a

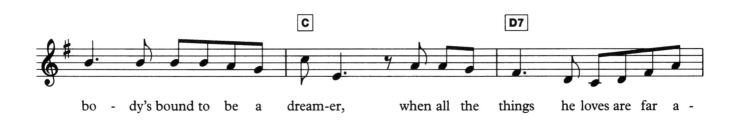

bo - dy's bound to be a dream-er, when all the things he loves are far a -

- way. And pre-cious things are dreams un - to an ex - ile, they take him

o'er the land a - cross the sea, es - pe - cially when it hap-pens he's an

ex - ile, from that dear love - ly Isle of In - nis - free. And when the

moon - light peeps a - cross the roof-tops of this great ci - ty, won-drous though it

be, I scarce-ly feel its won-der, or its laugh-ter, I'm once a -

- gain back home in In - nis - free._____

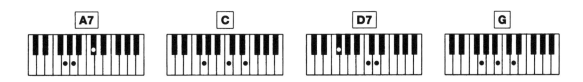

KILLARNEY

Words by E Falconer / Music by Balfe

Suggested Registration: Clarinet
Rhythm: Soft Rock
Tempo: ♩ = 92

1 By Killarney's lakes and fells,
   Em'rald isles and winding bays,
   Mountain paths and woodland dells.
   Mem'ry ever fondly strays,
   Bounteous nature loves all lands.
   Beauty wanders everywhere,
   Footprints leaves on many strands,
   But her home is surely there!
   Angels fold their wings, and rest
   In that Eden of the west,
   Beauty's home Killarney,
   Heavn's reflex Killarney.

2 No place else can charm the eye,
   With such bright and varied tints.
   Every rock that you pass by,
   Verdure broiders or besprints.
   Virgin there the green grass grows,
   Every morn spring's natal day;
   Bright hued berries daff the snows
   Smiling winter's frown away.
   Angels, often pausing there,
   Doubt if Eden were more fair;
   Beauty's home, Killarney,
   Heav'ns reflex, Killarney.

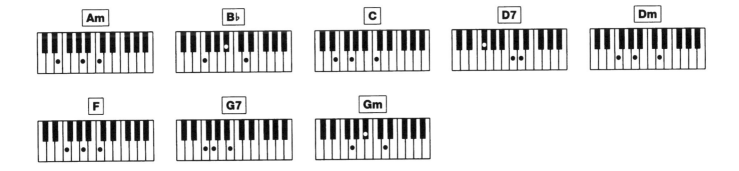

Let Him Go, Let Him Tarry

Traditional

Suggested Registration: Piano
Rhythm: Soft Rock
Tempo: ♩ = 100

Fare-well to cold win-ter, now that sum-mer's come at last.

no-thing have I gained,_ but my true love I have lost. I'll

sing and I'll be hap-py like the birds up-on the tree, for

since he de-ceived me I care no more for he. *Let him*

go, let him tar-ry, let him sink or let him swim.

He does-n't care for me, and I don't care for him. He can

go and get an - oth - er, that I hope he will en - joy, for

I'm going to mar - ry a far ni - cer boy.

1   Farewell to cold winter, now that summer's come at last.
      Nothing have I gained, but my true love I have lost.
      I'll sing and I'll be happy like the birds upon the tree,
      For since he deceived me I care no more for he.

Let him go, let him tarry,
Let him sink or let him swim.
He doesn't care for me, and I don't care for him.
He can go and get another, that I hope he will enjoy,
For I'm going to marry a far nicer boy.

2   He wrote me a letter, saying he was very bad,
      I sent him back an answer, saying I was awful glad.
      He wrote to me another, saying he was well and strong,
      But I care no more about him than the ground he walks upon.

Let him go . . .

3   Some of his friends had a good kind wish for me,
      Others of his friends, they could hang me on a tree;
      But soon I'll let them see my love, and soon I'll let them know,
      That I can get a new sweetheart on any ground I go.

Let him go . . .

4   He can go to his old mother now and set her mind at ease,
      I hear she is an old, old woman, very hard to please.
      It's slighting me and talking ill is what she's always done,
      Because that I was courting her great big ugly son.

Let him go . . .

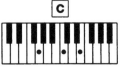
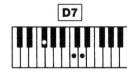
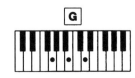

THE MINSTREL BOY

Words by Thomas Moore / Music traditional

Suggested Registration: Flute
Rhythm: Soft Rock
Tempo: ♩ = 100

The mins-trel boy___ to the war is gone, in the ranks of death_ you'll_ find him. His fa-ther's sword he has gird-ed on, and his wild harp slung_____ be-hind him. 'Land of song,' said the war-rior bard, 'Though all the world be-trays___ thee. One sword at least,_ thy___ rights shall guard. One_ faith-ful heart_____ shall praise thee!' The mins-trel fell,_ but the

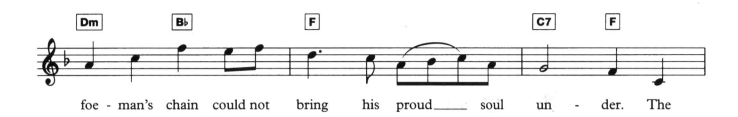

foe - man's chain could not bring his proud＿ soul un - der. The

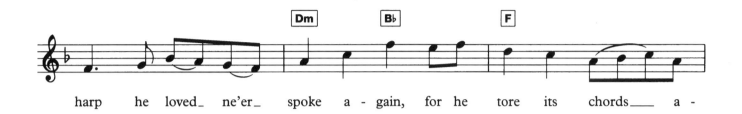

harp he loved＿ ne'er＿ spoke a - gain, for he tore its chords＿ a -

-sun - der, and said, 'No chain shall＿ sul - ly thee, thou

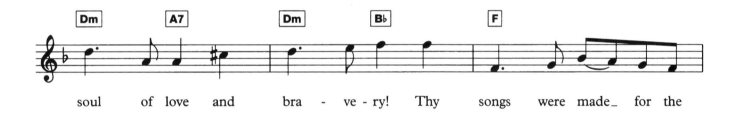

soul of love and bra - ve - ry! Thy songs were made＿ for the

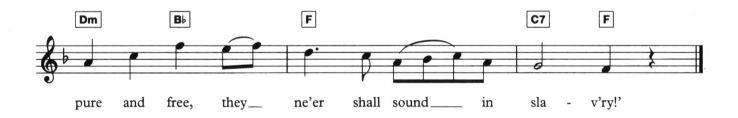

pure and free, they＿ ne'er shall sound＿ in sla - v'ry!'

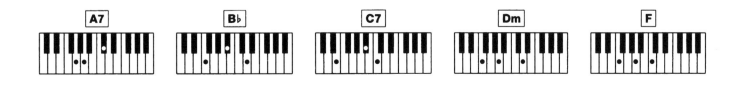

MOLLY MALONE
(COCKLES AND MUSSELS)

Traditional

Suggested Registration: Recorder V141 DV95 Final Chorus V105 Very Slow
Rhythm: Waltz S46 (T66)
Tempo: ♩ = 132

1 In Dublin's fair city,
   Where the girls are so pretty,
   I first set my eyes on sweet Molly Malone,
   As she wheeled her wheelbarrow,
   Through streets broad and narrow,
   Crying, 'Cockles and mussels! Alive, alive-o!'
   Alive, alive-o!
   Alive, alive-o!
   Crying, 'Cockles and mussels!
   Alive, alive-o!'

2 She was a fishmonger,
   But sure t'was no wonder,
   For so were her father and mother before,
   And they each wheeled their barrow,
   Through streets broad and narrow,
   Crying, 'Cockles and mussels! Alive, alive-o!'
   Alive, alive-o . . .

3 She died of a fever,
   And no one could save her,
   And that was the end of sweet Molly Malone,
   But her ghost wheels her barrow,
   Through streets broad and narrow,
   Crying, 'Cockles and mussels! Alive, alive-o!'
   Alive, alive-o . . .

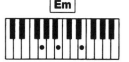
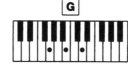

MOUNTAINS OF MOURNE

Words and Music by William Percy French

Suggested Registration: Accordian V35 D/H
Rhythm: Waltz
Tempo: ♩ = 160 S24(T160)

Oh Ma - ry, this Lon - don's a won - der - ful

sight, wid the peo - ple here work - in' by day and by

night. They don't sow po - ta - toes, nor bar - ley, nor

wheat, but there's gangs of them dig - gin' for gold in the

street. At least when I axed them, that's what I was

told, So, I just took a hand at this dig - gin' for

gold,   but   for   all   that   I   found   there,   I   might   as   well

be,   where the   moun-tains   of   Mourne   sweep   down   to   the   sea.

1   Oh Mary, this London's a wonderful sight,
Wid the people here workin' by day and by night.
They don't sow potatoes, nor barley, nor wheat,
But there's gangs of them diggin' for gold in the street.
At least when I axed them, that's what I was told,
So I just took a hand at this diggin' for gold,
But for all that I found there, I might as well be,
Where the mountains of Mourne sweep down to the sea.

2   I believe that when writin' a wish you expressed,
As to how the fine ladies in London were dressed.
Well, if you'll believe me when axed to a ball,
They don't wear a top to their dresses at all.
Oh, I've seen them myself, and you could not in thrath,
Say if they were bound for a ball or a bath.
Don't be startin' them fashions now, Mary Machree,
Where the mountains of Mourne sweep down to the sea.

4   You remember young Peter O'Loughlin of course?
Well he's over here at the head o' the Force.
I met him today, I was crossing the Strand,
And he stopped the whole street wid wan wave of his hand,
And there we stood talkin' of days that are gone,
While the whole population of London looked on,
But for all these great powers he's wishful like me,
To be back where dark Mourne sweeps down to the sea.

3   I seen England's King from the top of a bus,
I never knew him though he means to know us,
And though by the Saxon we once were oppressed,
Still I cheered, God forgive me! I cheered with the rest,
And now that he's visited Erin's green shore,
We'll be much better friends than we've been heretofore.
When we've got all we want we're as quiet can be,
Where the mountains of Mourne sweep down to the sea.

5   There's beautiful girls here, oh never you mind,
Wid beautiful shapes nature never designed,
An' lovely complexions all roses and crame,
But O'Loughlin remarked wid regard to them same,
'Since you're a foine feller, I'll give you a tip,
Them colours might all come away on your lip.'
So, I'll wait for the wild rose that's waitin' for me,
Where the mountains of Mourne sweep down to the sea.

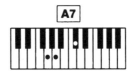 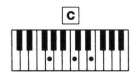 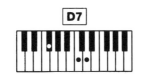 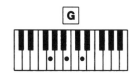

My Wild Irish Rose

Traditional

Suggested Registration: Violin V81 DV105
Rhythm: Waltz S12 (T128)
Tempo: ♩ = 128   S2 (T92) Irish Tenors

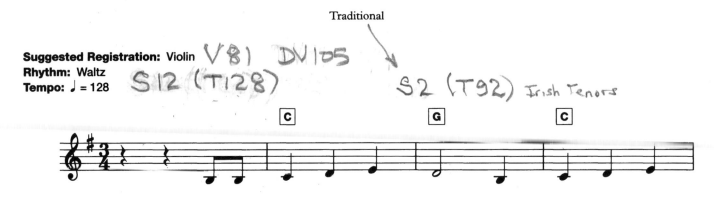

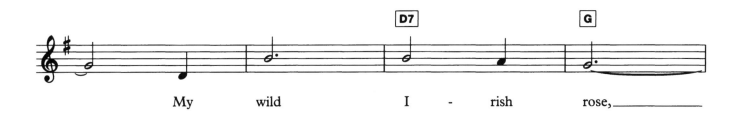

My wild I - rish rose,_____

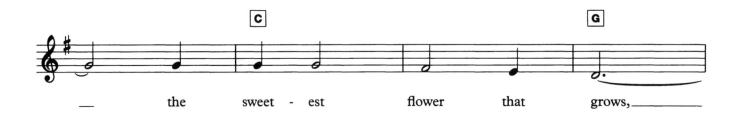

___ the sweet - est flower that grows,_____

___ you may search ev - ery - where, but none can com -

- pare with my wild I - rish rose._____

_ My wild I - rish rose,_____

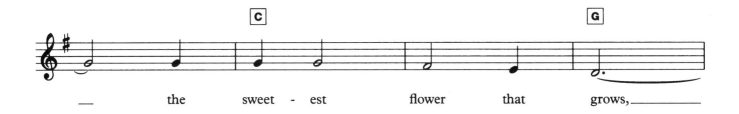

_ the sweet - est flower that grows,_____

_ and some - day, for my sake, she may let me

take the bloom from my wild I - rish rose._____

OH! ARRANMORE

Words by Moore / Music traditional

Suggested Registration: Flute V137 DN105
Rhythm: Soft Rock S99 (TT68)
Tempo: ♩ = 84

Oh!

Ar - ran-more, loved Ar - ran - more, how oft I dream of thee, and

of those days when by thy shore, I wan - dered young and free. Full

many a path I've tried since then, through plea - sure's flow - ery maze, but

ne'er could find the bliss a - gain, I felt in those sweet days.

1   Oh! Arranmore, loved Arranmore,
    How oft I dream of thee,
    And of those days when by thy shore,
    I wandered young and free.
    Full many a path I've tried since then,
    Through pleasure's flowery maze,
    But ne'er could find the bliss again,
    I felt in those sweet days.

2   How blithe upon thy breezy cliffs,
    At sunny morn I've stood,
    With heart, as bounding as the skiffs
    That danced along thy flood.
    Or when the western wave grew bright,
    With daylight's parting wing,
    Have sought that Eden in its light,
    Which dreaming poets sing.

3   That Eden, where th'immortal brave
    Dwell in a land serene,
    Whose bowers beyond the shining wave,
    At sunset oft are seen.
    Ah! Dream, too full of saddening truth,
    Those mansions o'er the main
    Are like the hopes I built in youth,
    As sunny and as vain!

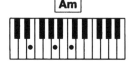
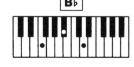
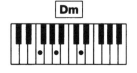
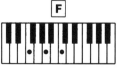
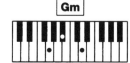

THE ROSE OF TRALEE

Words by E Mordaunt Spencer / Music by Charles W Glover

Suggested Registration: Acoustic Guitar
Rhythm: Waltz
Tempo: ♩ = 116

me. Oh no! 'Twas the truth in her eye ev - er

dawn - ing, that made me love Ma - ry, the rose of Tra - lee.

1 The pale moon was rising above the green mountain,
The sun was declining beneath the blue sea,
When I strayed with my love to the pure crystal fountain
That stands in the beautiful vale of Tralee.
She was lovely and fair as the rose of the summer,
Yet 'twas not her beauty alone that won me.
Oh no! 'Twas the truth in her eye ever dawning
That made me love Mary, the Rose of Tralee.

2 The cold shades of evening, their mantle were spreading,
And Mary all smiling was listening to me.
The moon through the valley, her pale rays was shedding,
When I won the heart of the rose of Tralee.
Though lovely and fair as the rose of summer,
Yet 'twas not her beauty alone that won me.
Oh no! 'Twas the truth in her eye ever dawning,
That made me love Mary, the Rose of Tralee.

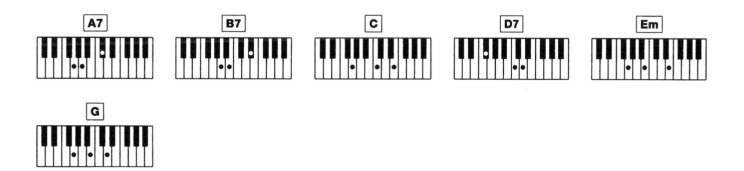

That's An Irish Lullaby

Words and Music by J R Shannon

Suggested Registration: Recorder
Rhythm: Slow Rock 6/8
Tempo: ♩. = 84

O - ver in Kil - lar - ney ____ ma - ny years a - go, ____ me

mi - ther sang a song to me, in tones so sweet and low. Just a

sim - ple lit - tle dit - ty, in her good ould I - rish way, and I

give the world, if she could sing that song to me this day. ____

Too - ra - loo - ra - loo - ral, ____ too - ra - loo - ra - li,

too - ra - loo - ra - loo - ral, ____ hush now, don't you cry! ____

Too - ra - loo - ra - loo - ral,   too - ra - loo - ra - li,

too - ra - loo - ra - loo - ral,   that's   an   I - rish lul - la - by.

1   Over in Killarney many years ago,
Me mither sang a song to me,
In tones so sweet and low.
Just a simple little ditty,
In her good ould Irish way,
And I give the world, if she could sing
That song to me this day.
    Too-ra-loo-ra-loo-ral,
    Too-ra-loo-ra-li,
    Too-ra-loo-ra-loo-ral,
    Hush now, don't you cry!
    Too-ra-loo-ra-loo-ral,
    Too-ra-loo-ra-li,
    Too-ra-loo-ra-loo-ral,
    That's an Irish lullaby.

2   Oft in dreams I wander to that cot again,
I feel her arms a-huggin' me,
As when she held me then,
And I hear her voice a-hummin' to me,
As in days of yore,
When she used to rock me fast asleep,
Outside the cabin door.
    Too-ra-loo-ra-loo-ral . . .

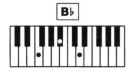
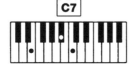
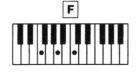

The Wearin' O' The Green

Traditional

Suggested Registration: Accordian
Rhythm: Soft Rock
Tempo: ♩ = 96

Oh, Pad - dy dear, and did ye hear the news that's go - in' round? The sham - rock is by law for - bid to grow on I - rish ground! No__ more Saint Pat - rick's Day we'll keep, his col - our can't be seen, for there's a cru - el law a - g'in the wear - in' o' the green. I__ met with Nap - per Tan - dy, and he took me by the hand, and he

said, 'How's poor ould Ire - land, and how___ does she stand?' 'She's the

most dis - tress - ful coun - try that ev - er yet was seen, for they're

hang - ing men and wo - men there, for the wear - in' o' the green.'

1   Oh, Paddy dear, and did ye hear the news that's goin' round?
    The shamrock is by law forbid to grow on Irish ground!
    No more Saint Patrick's Day we'll keep, his colour can't be seen,
    For there's a cruel law ag'in the wearin' o' the green.
    I met with Napper Tandy, and he took me by the hand,
    And he said, 'How's poor ould Ireland, and how does she stand?'
    'She's the most distressful country that ever yet was seen,
    For they're hanging men and women there, for the wearin' o' the green.'

2   'So if the colour we must wear be England's cruel red,
    Let it remind us of the blood that Irishmen have shed,
    And pull the shamrock from your hat, and throw it on the sod,
    But never fear 'twill take root there though underfoot 'tis trod.
    When laws can stop the blades of grass from growin' as they grow,
    And when the leaves in summer-time their colour dare not show,
    Then I will change the colour too I wear in my caubeen,
    But till that day, please God, I'll stick to the wearin' o' the green.'

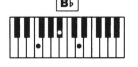
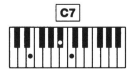
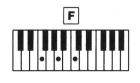

WHEN IRISH EYES ARE SMILING

Words by Chauncy Olcott and Geo Graff Jr / Music by Ernest R Ball

Suggested Registration: Accordian
Rhythm: Waltz
Tempo: ♩ = 184

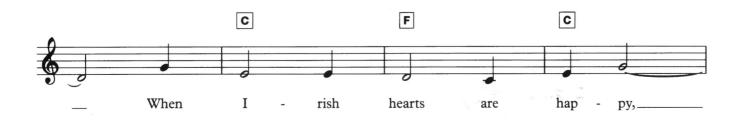

When I - rish hearts are hap - py, _____

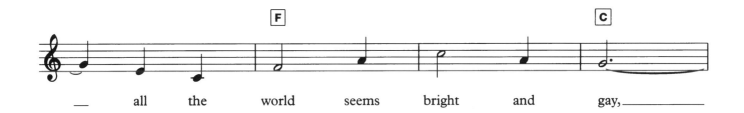

_ all the world seems bright and gay, _____

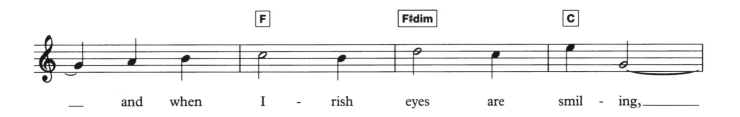

_ and when I - rish eyes are smil - ing, _____

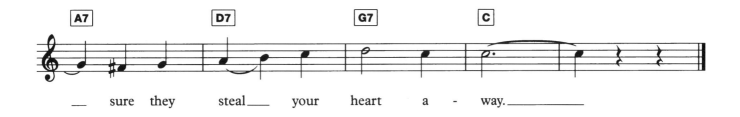

_ sure they steal _ your heart a - way. _____

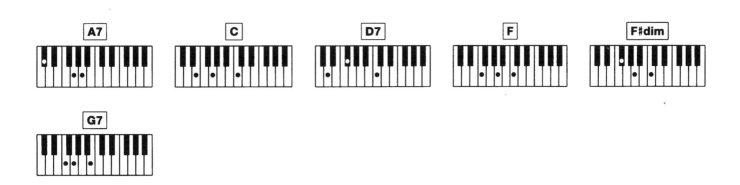

THE WILD ROVER

Traditional

Suggested Registration: Accordian
Rhythm: Waltz
Tempo: ♩ = 160

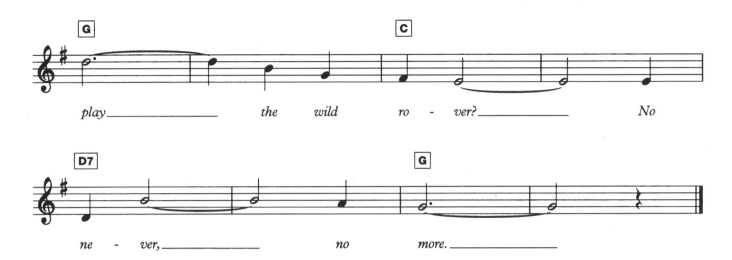

play_____ the wild ro - ver?_____ No

ne - ver,_____ no more._____

1 I've been a wild rover for many a year,
 And I've spent all my money on whiskey and beer,
 But now I'm returning with gold in great store,
 And I never will play the wild rover no more.
  And it's no, nay, never,
  No, nay, never no more,
  Will I play the wild rover,
  No never, no more.

2 I went into an ale house I used to frequent,
 And I told the landlady my money was spent.
 I asked for a bottle: she answered me, 'Nay,
 Such a custom as yours I can get any day.'
  And it's no, nay . . .

3 Then out of my pocket I took sovereigns bright,
 And the landlady's eyes opened wide with delight.
 She said, 'I have whiskies and wines of the best,
 And the words that I said, sure, were only in jest.'
  And it's no, nay . . .

4 I'll go back to my parents, confess what I've done,
 And ask them to pardon their prodigal son.
 And if they caress me as oftimes before,
 Then I never will play the wild rover no more.
  And it's no, nay . . .

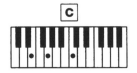 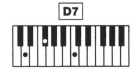 

Printed and bound in Great Britain by Caligraving Limited

The Easy Keyboard Library

An expansive series of over 50 titles!

Each song features melody line, vocals, chord displays, suggested registrations and rhythm settings.

*"For each title ALL the chords (both 3 finger and 4 finger) used
are shown in the correct position – which makes a change!"*
Organ & Keyboard Cavalcade

Each song appears on two facing pages,
eliminating the need to turn the page during performance.

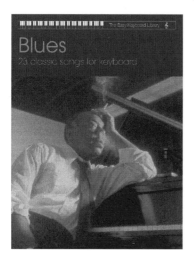
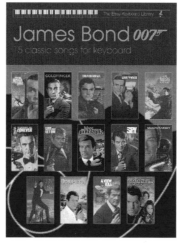

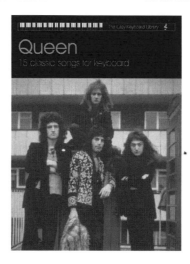

To buy Faber Music publications or to find out about the full range of titles available
please contact your local music retailer or Faber Music sales enquiries:

Faber Music Ltd, Burnt Mill, Elizabeth Way, Harlow CM20 2HX
Tel: +44 (0) 1279 82 89 82   Fax: +44 (0) 1279 82 89 83
sales@fabermusic.com   fabermusic.com   expressprintmusic.com